Jesus Brings Us Life

by Sister Anne Eileen Heffernan, FSP
with
Sister Anne Joan Flanagan, FSP

This book belongs to

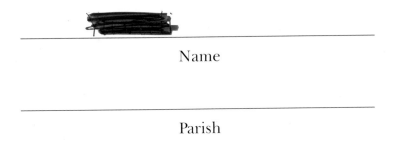

_____

Name

_____

Parish

With this book I am preparing for two great sacraments!

Pauline
BOOKS & MEDIA

Nihil Obstat: Rev. Paul M. Parker, STL
Imprimatur: ✠ Bernard Cardinal Law
September 27, 1995

Special Consultants

Rev. Stephen F. Brett, SSJ—moral
Rev. Thomas W. Buckley—biblical, theological
Lois Butler—pedagogical
Sister Diane Carollo, MSBT—pastoral, cultural
David Heller—psychological
Rev. Fernando Hernandez—pastoral
Richard J. Lynch—pedagogical
Helen Maldini—pedagogical
Alfred McBride, O.Praem.—theological, pedagogical
Madeleine A. McCarty—pastoral, pedagogical
Gloria McCasland—pedagogical
Bea Monaghan—pastoral
Jane Murphy—pedagogical
Maria Elena Pacheco-Aguilera—cultural
Rev. Ed Ryan—pastoral
Celia M. Sirois—biblical, pedagogical
Rev. John P. Tackney—pastoral, pedagogical
Susan Wessel—pedagogical

Editing

Staff, Pauline Books & Media

Design

Sister Mary Joseph Peterson, FSP
Sister Tracey Matthia Dugas, FSP

Photos

Sister Mary Emmanuel Alves, FSP: 9, 22, 36, 37, 46, 52, 70, 82, 109, 117, 152, 153
Sister Sergia Ballini, FSP: 19
John Capobianco: 98, 119
Sister Maria Agnes Cremòn: 7
Giancarlo Giuliani: 66
Sister Ancilla Christine Hirsch, FSP: 52
Christine Noell: 52
FSP: 25, 56, 70

Illustrations

Cover: Dick Smolinski
Biblical Illustrations: Keith Neely
Contemporary Illustrations: Virginia Esquinaldo
Activity Pages: Elizabeth Ann Keating

Bartolomé Esteban Murillo,
The Return of the Prodigal Son: 63

"The Ad Hoc Committee to Oversee the Use of the *Catechism* of the National Conference of Catholic Bishops has found this catechetical text to be in conformity with the *Catechism of the Catholic Church*."

The authors and publishers also wish to express their gratitude to the members of several archdiocesan/diocesan staffs and other religious educators who have so kindly reviewed drafts of this program and have given such valuable input.

ISBN 0-1898-3960-4

Published by Pauline Books & Media, 50 Saint Pauls Avenue, Boston MA 02130-3491.

www.pauline.org.

Printed in Korea.

JBUL SIPSKOGUNKYO8-26043 3960-4

Pauline Books & Media is the publishing house of the Daughters of St. Paul, an international congregation of women religious serving the Church with the communications media.

10 11 12 13 14   19 18 17 16 15

Contents

PART 1
We Belong to God's Family

1. God Is Close to Us 6
2. God Speaks to Us 12
3. The Holy Spirit Helps 18

4. We Share God's Life 24
5. Signs of God's Presence 30
6. God Likes to Hear Us 36

PART 2
Jesus Helps Us Live God's Way

7. We Learn God's Ways 44
8. We Love Each Other 50
9. We Enjoy God's World 56
10. We Need God's Help 62
11. God Gives Us Peace 68

12. God Helps Us Get Ready 74
13. God and the Church
    Welcome Us 80
14. We Learn to Do Better 86

PART 3
Jesus Gives Himself to Us

15. We Give Thanks with Jesus 94
16. Easter Is Our
    Biggest Celebration 100
17. Jesus Is with Us at Mass 106
18. We Live by God's Word 112

19. Jesus Is Our Gift to God 118
20. Jesus Is Our
    Holy Communion 124
21. Jesus Teaches Us to Pray 130
22. Pentecost Is a Day of Joy 136

SPECIAL SESSIONS

Jesus Is Coming 144
We Grow in Lent 146
How to Celebrate
the Sacrament of Penance 148

What We See and Do at Mass 152
Let's Talk to God 156
Glossary 158

e are God's children now.

(1 John 3:2)

Part One
We Belong to God's Family

God Is Close to Us

We Share

Did you ever wait for a special person to come to your house? Or did you ever wait for a special day, like your birthday?

We Listen

Sometimes people feel lonely. They feel like they are waiting for something or someone. They feel empty. Do you know why? All of us were made to be happy with God.

God may seem far away, but God is really with us. The Bible says, "Lord, you are all around me on every side" (Ps. 139:1, 5). God loves us very much. God cares about everything that happens in our lives.

God can do anything. God made the sun, the moon and the stars. God made animals and people. God made everything in the world. And it was good.

God gave us special gifts. God made us able to think, to love and to make choices. Using these gifts in the right way will help us to be happy with God forever.

This year, we will learn how to use God's gifts in the right way. And this year we will move even closer to God.

7

St. Francis Praises
God Our Maker

We Choose

Choose one of these lines to learn by heart. Say it to at least one other person.

God loves *me* very much.

God loves *us* very much.

God cares about everything.

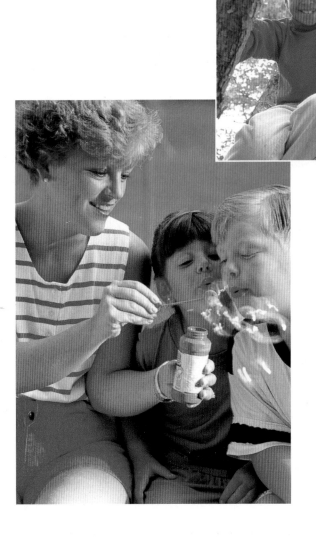

We Grow

I can talk to God with this prayer from the Bible:

O Lord, our God, how great you are!
I look at the sky which you have made
and the moon and stars which you put there.
How good you are to think about us!
How good you are to take care of us!

(Psalm 8)

10

God Gave Us Special Gifts.

We can think and know.

We can love.

In the notebook, write something you know about from religion class.

In the heart, draw a picture of someone who loves you.

We can make choices.

What would you choose if you were Dana?

God Speaks to Us

We Share

Logan's mother gave him a message. "Tell Evan to come set the table." Logan went to Evan's room. "Mom said to come set the table."

Do you ever get messages this way?

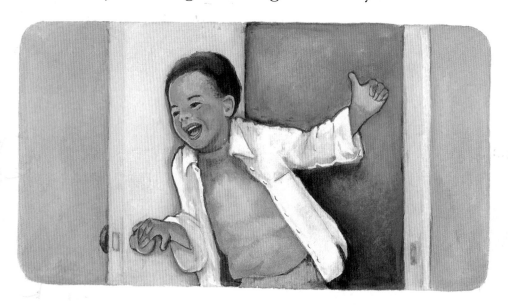

We Listen

God is different from us. We cannot see God or hear God. How can God talk to us?

God can speak to us in our hearts.

A long time ago, God spoke to some people in their hearts. He acted in their lives. God told them how to live. These people wrote down God's message. That was how the Bible began. The Bible is like a long letter from God to us.

Then God spoke to us in another way. The Bible says, "God has spoken to us through his Son" (Heb. 1:1).

God's Son is Jesus. Jesus is God, like his Father. He always was God. But he also became human like us.

Jesus *showed* people how to live as God wants. He was good to everyone! He taught them about God's love. He asked them to love each other. Jesus said and did all this for *us,* too. People wrote it down. We can read it in the Bible.

Jesus loves us very much. He died on the cross to save us. God the Father raised Jesus from the dead. Jesus is alive! He wants us to live with him and his Father forever.

SARAH

ABRAHAM

ISAAC

MOSES

RUTH

JESUS

Jesus Teaches about God's Love.

Jesus showed people how to live. He taught them about God's love.

Draw the crowds who listened to Jesus. Put yourself there, too!

14

We Choose

Name three ways you can hear or read
God's word.
Which way is best for you?
Which can you do every day?

Pray

go to church

We Grow

Jesus gave God's message to the whole world. Now it is our turn to share it with others.

B

St. Paula learned about the Bible from a great teacher, St. Jerome. St. Paula's example and knowledge led other people to pray with God's Word.

Follow the dots to finish the picture!

The Holy Spirit Helps

We Share

When you have to do something hard, who helps you?

We Listen

Sometimes it is hard for us to do the right thing. Sometimes we do not even know what is right and good. So God sends the Holy Spirit to help us.

The Holy Spirit is God, like God the Father, and like God the Son. We cannot see or hear the Holy Spirit, but the Spirit can speak to us in our hearts.

God the Father raised Jesus from the dead because God loves Jesus and us. God wanted to share his very life with us. The Holy Spirit brought us the life of God when we were baptized. That life is called grace. The Spirit made us members of the Church—the family of Jesus.

The Bible says, "God's love is poured into our hearts by the Holy Spirit" (Rom. 5:5). The Spirit

helps us to love God and each other the way Jesus does.

The Holy Spirit helps us to do good things. The Spirit helps us to know when we have done something wrong.

Jesus and the Holy Spirit want God's life to grow in us. This year Jesus and the Holy Spirit invite us to receive the sacraments of Penance and Eucharist. Jesus and the Spirit invite us to grow closer to them and to all God's people.

This is my beloved Son.
My favor rests on him.

Find the hidden dove, a
symbol of the Holy Spirit.

We Choose

The Bible says, "The Spirit prays in us, saying 'Father!'" (Gal. 4:6).

In the morning, you can ask God the Father to send the Holy Spirit to help you all day long!

At night, you can thank the Father, Son and Holy Spirit for being with you, day and night.

We Grow

Even though we cannot see the Holy Spirit, some pictures help us think of the Holy Spirit. Have you seen any of these in church?

B Circle the words you find in the puzzle.
Cross them off the list as you find them.

```
A  B  C  F  D  E
F  G  R  A  C  E
S  O  N  T  H  I
J  D  K  H  L  M
N  O  P  E  Q  R
S  P  I  R  I  T
```

FATHER
SON
SPIRIT
GRACE
GOD

We Share God's Life

We Share

Think of a happy time you had with other people. Who were you with? What made you so happy? Whom did you tell about your happy time?

We Listen

God the Father and God the Son and God the Holy Spirit love everybody in the world. They want all people to be happy with them. They want God's people, the Church, to tell everybody else the good news of God's love, the way you want to tell others about your happy times.

Jesus says to God's people, "Go out into the whole world and tell the good news to all people. Baptize them in the name of the Father and of the Son and of the Holy Spirit. Teach them everything I taught you. I will always be with you—till the end of the world" (Mt. 28:19-20).

People join the Church by being baptized. Baptism is a sacrament. A sacrament is a celebration of the Church in which the Holy Spirit shares God's life with us.

Can you name two other sacraments?

When we were baptized the Holy Spirit did wonderful things for us. The Spirit made us children of the Father by giving us a share in God's life. The Spirit came to live in us and joined us to Jesus. The Spirit made us members of the Church.

What a great event our baptism was!

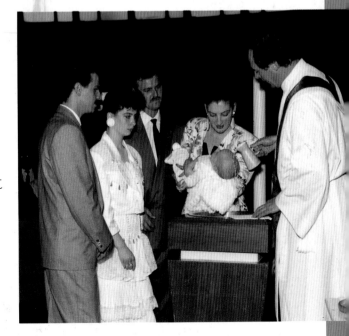

God Lives in Us!

Pour the water of baptism over the baby's head.

Say: I baptize you in the Name of the Father and of the Son and of the Holy Spirit.

We Choose

You can renew your baptismal promises!

We Grow

What is the Church doing?

Renewal of Baptismal Promises

_____

Name

I turn away from sin.
I believe in God, the Father almighty,
creator of heaven and earth.
I believe in Jesus Christ,
his only Son, our Lord.
I believe in the Holy Spirit
and the Catholic Church.

God gave me new life in baptism
and took away all sin.
May God keep me faithful forever.

_____

Date

_____

Witness

Signs of God's Presence

We Share

When Jesus went around teaching, he looked very ordinary. But sometimes he would do something special. Do you know about any of the special things that Jesus did?

We Listen

Jesus made sick people well. He made deaf people hear. He walked on the sea. He changed water into wine.

One day Jesus saw a man who had been blind all his life. Jesus wanted the man to be able to see. To cure him, Jesus put mud on the man's eyes. Then he told him to go wash away the mud in a pool. The man did it and he was cured! "I went and I washed and I saw!" he said. He was very happy.

These wonderful things that Jesus did are called *miracles*. They showed that Jesus had the power of God. They showed that Jesus cares about people and wants them to be happy.

Jesus still does wonderful things today. He does them in the sacraments. When he cured the blind man, Jesus used mud and asked the man to use water. In the seven sacraments, certain members of God's people act for Jesus. They use water, oil, bread and wine. They say special words. When they do, the Holy Spirit makes God's life grow in us and in the whole Church!

How many sacraments have you received? Which sacrament will you receive next?

Jesus Makes the Blind Man See

Number the pictures in order. The first one is done for you. Then use the word clues to tell the story to another person. Be sure to tell them what the mud was for.

3 Mud.

Wash.

4 See!

1 Blind.

Name three things the Church uses in the sacraments.

5 I believe!

We Choose

God's life and love are meant to be shared. Explain to another person why you are preparing to receive the sacraments.

We Grow

Not everyone who met Jesus got a miracle, but everyone heard the message of God's love. Sing a song about Jesus showing God's care for us!

Jesus Feeds the Big Crowd

Put bread or a fish in every person's hand.

God Likes to Hear Us

We Share

When you go to play at a friend's house, do you want your friend to leave you by yourself? How would you feel if your friend did that?

We Listen

God is a friend who is always with us. It is good for us to remember this. Sometimes we talk to God. Thinking about God or talking and listening to God is called *prayer.*

Jesus showed us how important prayer is. When Jesus was alone, he used to talk to God his Father. When he was with other people, he often prayed with them. Sometimes they would sing prayer-songs called *psalms.* The psalms are prayers from the Bible. We say or sing some psalms at Mass.

When we pray, we can thank God for being so great and so good. We can say how much we love God. We can tell God that we are sorry for anything bad we have done. And we can ask God to help us with the problems that we have. The Bible says: "Pray whenever you can" (Eph. 6:18).

We can pray to Mary, too. Mary is Jesus' mother. Because Jesus is God, Mary is the Mother of God. When we pray to Mary, she prays to Jesus for us.

A Use the word clues to fill in the puzzle.
The first one is done for you.

pray   sorrow   ask   adore   thank

Down

1. "I like to talk with God," said Erin.
   "I like to P R A Y."

3. To praise God with love. _a d o r e_

Across

4. We pray with _s o r r o w_ over the harm
   caused by sin.

5. _t h a n k_ you, God, for your goodness
   to me!

2. We can _a s k_ God for what we need.

De-Code: God loves to hear our P Y E R R A.

_p r a y e r_

We Choose

How do you pray in church?

How do you pray at home?

Where else do you pray?

We Grow

Alex was sad. His best friend was moving to a new house. It was far away.

Mom said, "I know this is hard. You can tell God how you feel."

Alex is not so sure you can talk to God when you are sad.

What can you tell Alex?

Jesus and Mary were at a wedding. The wine ran out. Mary told Jesus about it. She told the people to do what Jesus said. Jesus told them, "Fill those big jars with water."
They did.
Jesus said, "Pour some into a cup."
When they did, the water had become wine. It was Jesus' first miracle. People began to believe in Jesus.

Fill the jars with water. (Color them *blue*.)
Show that Jesus made the water into wine. (Use red *over* the blue.)

ove each
other
as I loved
you.
(John 15:12)

Part Two
Jesus Helps Us Live God's Way

We Learn God's Ways

We Share

Garth has a photo of his grandpa. In what ways is the photo like Garth's grandpa? In what ways is the photo different?

We Listen

A photo is an *image.* An image is something that looks like something else, but there are always great differences, too.

The Bible says, "God made human beings...in his image" (Wis. 2:23). This means that we are a little like God. God knows everything. We know some things. God loves everybody. We try to love everybody. God always does what is good. We try to do only good things.

The Father, Jesus and the Holy Spirit want us to become more like them. They want us to get ready to be happy with them forever. That is why God has given us the ten commandments. They are rules for living the right way.

God helps us to know and to do what is good. When we live God's way, we become better images of God!

These are the first three commandments:

1. I am the Lord your God: you shall not have strange gods before me.

2. You shall not take the name of the Lord your God in vain.

3. Remember to keep holy the Lord's Day.

By keeping (obeying) these first three commandments, we do what the Bible asks us to do where it says: "You shall love the Lord your God with all your heart, with all your soul, with all your mind, and with all your strength" (Mk. 12:30).

The first commandment tells us to learn about God, to love God and to pray to God.

The second commandment tells us to respect God's name. We say "God" or "Jesus" only in love and respect, not when we are surprised or angry.

The third commandment tells us that Sunday is special. Sunday is the Lord's Day (God's Day). It is a day to spend some time with God. Sunday is a day when people can enjoy family, relax and do good things for others. And Sunday (or Saturday night) is the time when we meet with God's family at Mass to pray and worship God together.

These first three commandments are all about God and us. They help us to love God our Father the way Jesus did.

If the action/choice matches the way to happiness, circle the tablets, if not, put an X through them.

Brendan crashed into Lolita's bike. "I'm sorry," Brendan said. "Are you okay?"

Keisha got up early on Sunday and went to Mass with her grandpa.

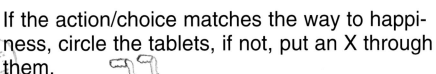

Renald forgot to do his homework. But he told the teacher that Matthew took it.

When Jesse goes to the nursing home to see Aunt Sharon, he always visits Mrs. Lowe, too. She has no family left to visit her.

Hong threw dirty clothes all over his sister's room to get her angry.

We Choose

Name the grown-ups who help you come to church and religion class.

Today, thank them for helping you learn and keep God's commandments.

We Grow

How can keeping God's commandments help us be more like God?

Why are God's commandments so important?

48

God gave us the commandments through Moses. Help Moses bring the commandments to the people. Pick up the letters on the way and use them to finish the message at the bottom of the page.

START→

FINISH!

I AM THE ____ ____ ____ ____ YOUR

____ ____ ____ : YOU SHALL NOT HAVE

___ ___ ___ ___ ___ ___ ___ ___ GODS

BEFORE ____ ____ .

Lesson 8

We Love Each Other

We Share

God loves you. Do you love Jesus?
Do you love yourself?

We Listen

God wants us to love ourselves. God also
wants us to love other people. God loves everybody.
The first three commandments are about
loving God. The other seven are about loving
ourselves and others. The Bible says, "You shall
love your neighbor as yourself" (Mk. 12:31).

Somebody once asked Jesus, "Who is my neighbor?" Jesus answered by telling a story. A man was hurt by robbers and was left on the street. Somebody came by but didn't stop. Somebody else came by and didn't stop either. Finally a man stopped and helped the one who was hurt. This man was from another country.

With this story, Jesus was telling us, "Your neighbor is everybody." In fact, all people are our *brothers and sisters,* because we all have one Father in heaven: God!

We Choose

TV and movies can give people ideas about how to treat others. Some of those ideas are good. Some are bad. What are some of the *good* ways TV can show people treating others?

We Grow

Make up a story for a TV show in which people treat others with respect.

Name of program

Written by _____

_____

Producer _____

Director _____

Costume Designer _____

Cameras _____

_____

_____

What is your show about?

_____

_____

When will it be shown?

_____   _____
DAY   TIME

Lesson 9
We Enjoy God's World

We Share

Of all the things that you have, which one do you like the most?

We Listen

God planned for people to own things. God likes us to enjoy the world and what is in it. There are commandments about this.

Here are the last four commandments:

7. You shall not steal.
8. You shall not bear false witness against your neighbor.
9. You shall not covet your neighbor's wife.
10. You shall not covet your neighbor's goods.

The seventh commandment tells us to take good care of what we have, including our pets. It also tells us not to damage anything, whether it belongs to us or not.

God gave us the world to enjoy and to keep beautiful for other people. It is wrong to litter streets and sidewalks or yards, parks or fields.

The seventh commandment tells us not to rob or steal, or even keep anything that belongs to someone else, unless that person really doesn't mind. Anybody who steals something has to give it back or pay for it.

Once, Jesus went to visit a man named Zaccheus. Zaccheus had been taking money that did not belong to him. When Jesus came to see him,

Zaccheus felt sad about the wrong he had done. He knew that Jesus was very good. So Zaccheus promised, "I will pay back four times as much as I have taken from others." Zaccheus said something else that pleased Jesus very much: "I will give half of my things to poor people."

Zaccheus came to understand God's ways.

The eighth commandment is about telling the truth.

It is wrong to tell a lie. It is wrong to cheat, too, because cheating is like saying that we deserve a better grade than we really do. It is wrong to tell lies about other people. Anybody who tells that kind of lie has to try to make up by admitting the truth.

The ninth and tenth commandments are about what we set our hearts on having. These commandments will be easier to understand later on.

God is so good to us! God has given us such good rules to live by!

Blessed Titus Brandsma

Blessed Titus was a priest. He was in charge of a Catholic newspaper. There was a war. Father Titus' paper told people the truth about the war. Some people did not like what Father Titus wrote. Father Titus did not stop telling and writing the truth. God gave him the courage to stand up for what is right.

We Choose

Kara wants to help children in a poor place. She outgrew her first Bible story book. Now it belongs to her little brother

- Can Kara give the book to the poor?
- Why or why not?
- What can Kara do?
- What would you do?

We Grow

What things would be different in the world if everyone lived by God's commandments?

A Prayer

1. God, you have given us many good

   ___Things___.
   HIGTNS

2. We want to ___share___ these things
   RASHE
   with other people.

3. Help us to respect all ___people___.
   LEOPPE

4. You gave us your own ___Son___ to teach and
   ONS
   save us.

5. You gave us a ___share___ in your own life.
   RASHE

6. You gave us a beautiful ___world___ to live in.
   LWORD

7. Help us to ___respect___ the environment.
   SPERCTE

8. Help us to respect the ___truth___. Amen.
   RUTHT

We Need God's Help

We Share

We are able to *make choices*—to decide what to do or not do. What are some choices you have made today?

We Listen

God gave us freedom. With our freedom we can show our love for God, for ourselves and for others by choosing good things to say and do. If, instead, we choose to say or do bad things, we harm our friendship with God and with the Church. We harm ourselves. And we harm others.

We are always free to say "No" to what is bad, but sometimes it is hard. It isn't God's fault that this is hard. The first people did not have trouble doing what was good and right. But then they listened to an angel who had turned away from God. This bad angel, called Satan (the devil), told our first parents a lie about God. They stopped trusting God. Then our first parents disobeyed God.

From that time on, our first parents often found it hard to say "Yes" to God and "No" to what is bad. We have the same trouble. Sometimes right choices are hard for us. We have to pray for God's help. The Bible says: "God will not let you be tempted beyond your strength" (1 Cor. 10:13).

If we feel like doing something bad and decide to do it, that is a sin. When we commit sin, we put our selfishness ahead of God. Selfishness is not real love for ourselves. It harms us. If a sin is very bad it breaks our friendship with God and God's family.

But God knows that we are weak. He sent Jesus to make up for the harm that our sins do. God will forgive our sins if we are sorry and say so.

A very special way to be forgiven by God the Father and Jesus is to receive the sacrament of Penance, also called Reconciliation. In this sacrament the priest speaks for Jesus and tells us that our sins have been forgiven.

The sacrament of Penance is like a gift from Jesus to us!

A Draw a gift box around choices that Jesus would make.

Cross out choices that do not match God's plan.

Disobey.

Care for the earth.

Pray at bedtime.

Forgive.

Tell the truth.

GOD'S PLAN

Love God above all.

Love each other.

Praise God.

Get even.

Help at home.

Clean your room.

Say morning prayers.

Waste a lot.

Tell lies to stay out of trouble.

Help little kids.

Break things on purpose.

Mess things up.

Take things that are not yours.

Thank God.

Say mean words.

Cheat in school.

Hit people who are ugly.

Pray at Mass.

We Choose

Why do we need God's commandments? How can God's commandments make a difference in the choices and decisions we make?

We Grow

What does it mean to *forgive* someone?

Remember a time when you forgave someone for what they did or said.

- How did the person ask your forgiveness?
- What happened next?

Circle the words that go with each story.

Marco hit Paul.
Now Marco wants to be friends again.
What should he say?

I'm sorry.   I forgive you.

Binh disobeyed his mother.
He knew it was wrong. Now he is sorry he did not obey. What can Binh say?

I'm sorry.   I forgive you.

Elsa broke Maria's skates on purpose. She is sorry. She told Maria, "What I did was wrong."
What can Maria say?

I'm sorry.    I forgive you.

Rosa wants to be more like Jesus. She is sorry for her sins. When she celebrates the sacrament of Penance, what does Jesus say?

I'm sorry.   I forgive you.

67

To help us remember that Penance reconciles us with the Church, we may celebrate the sacrament in a group. We can pray and sing together and listen to readings from the Bible. There may be a talk by a priest or somebody else. Then there will be quiet time so we can remember our sins. After that we will have a chance to go to confession one by one in the reconciliation room or confessional. At the end, we might pray and sing together again.

This way of receiving Penance and Reconciliation helps us remember that we are all children of God our Father and brothers and sisters of each other. We belong to God's family.

St. Peter

Peter was Jesus' follower. But one day, Peter told a big lie. He said he did not even know Jesus. He said it three times. Jesus looked at Peter. Peter started to cry. Jesus wanted to forgive Peter. When Peter saw Jesus again, Jesus said, "Do you love me?" Peter said yes. He said it three times. Peter's love made up for the lies.

How did Peter answer Jesus? Write it in the spaces.

We Choose

When you pray at night, be sure to thank God for the good things of the day. See how you spent the day. God helped you do many good things. You can thank God with a prayer like this:

"Give thanks to the Lord, for he is good!" (Ps. 118:1).

Quietly "confess" to God the choices you made that did not match his commandments. Ask God's forgiveness for your sins. The "Jesus prayer" is a good prayer for this:

Lord Jesus, Son of God, have mercy on me, a sinner.

We Grow

What is happening?

72

Cross out every B and X and you will find a hidden message!

BIN PEXNANCEB
BWEXX FIBND XFOBRGIVENESS
FORB XOUR SINBS
XFROBM XGBOD BAND THEX
CHURCHB

In penance we find forgiveness for our sins from god and the church.

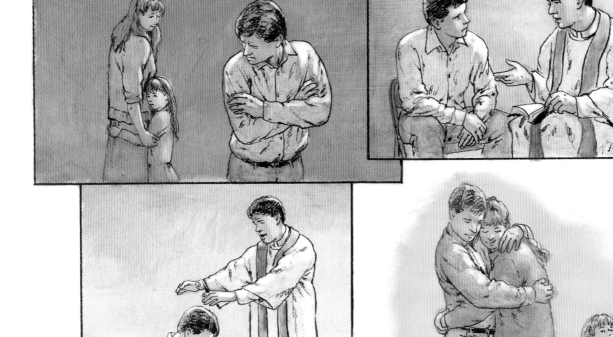

God Helps Us Get Ready

We Share

Name some things you do to get ready:

- when you go to Mass
- when you have a test at school
- when you have a birthday party
- for a big game

We Listen

When we have something important to do, we need to get ready. This is true about confession, too. We need to remember the wrong things that we have done—the things that were sins. We can ask God to help us remember. (We can ask an older person whom we trust, too, until we get used to doing this.)

One day, Jesus was eating in the house of a man named Simon. A woman came in. This woman had done bad things and she was sorry. She knew

that Jesus was good and kind. She started to cry.

We do not have to cry when we get ready for confession. But we have to be sorry for our sins and dislike them. We should decide not to commit them again. If this is hard, we can remember that Jesus suffered and died because of our sins. When we love Jesus, it is easier to be sorry for our sins.

Some sins are worse than others. Really bad sins are called "mortal" sins. A mortal sin is something really terrible, which a person knows is bad, and thinks about and chooses anyway. Most sins are less bad. They are called "venial" sins.

The woman at Simon's house got down on her knees next to Jesus and washed his feet with her tears. Her actions showed that she was sorry for her sins. Jesus was very kind to the woman. He told her that her sins had been forgiven, because she loved God.

Even if somebody has committed a very bad sin, God will forgive that person if the person is sorry for being unkind to God, who loves us so much. But through the Church, God asks people to tell every mortal sin in confession, too. They can be happy to do it, because in confession, they know they have been forgiven.

A Which can help you get ready to confess your sins?

☐ Remember sins.

☒ Don't do anything. Just talk.

☑ Decide not to commit sins.

☒ Eat an ice cream cone.

☑ Be truly sorry for the wrong you have done.

☒ Polish school shoes.

☑ Ask God to help you remember your sins.

☒ Pretend you never do wrong things.

We Choose

You can start now to get ready for your first confession. If it is hard for you to know what can be a sin, the questions on pages 148 and 149 may help you.

We Grow

Imagine you are the woman who met Jesus at Simon's house. How would you feel as you went home that day? What would you do the next time you saw Jesus?

Three to Get Ready

In the middle fingers, write three steps that help you prepare for the sacrament of Penance. Later, your teacher will name two more steps in a good confession.

rmender you sins

ask good for help

Threuly sory

God and the Church Welcome Us

We Share

Did you ever disobey a caring adult and try to hide it? How did you feel? Did you say something about it later?

We Listen

When we have disobeyed, we usually feel better after we say what we did and apologize for it. That's the way God made us. So when we have disobeyed God's commandments, we feel better after we have said it in confession. In confession we tell our sins to the priest and also to God, because God our Father, Jesus and the Holy Spirit are right there with us.

Jesus told a beautiful story about God's forgiveness.

There was a boy who asked his father for a lot of money and then ran away from home with it. Soon the boy had spent all the money. The only job he could get was feeding pigs. There was almost nothing to eat. At last the boy decided to go home and work for his father.

When the boy saw his father, he said, "Father, I have displeased God and hurt you. I'm sorry. Let me be one of your workers." The father hugged him and gave a big party for him. He was so happy to have his son home again!

God is the same way with us. When we tell the priest what we have done wrong, God is happy "to have us back home."

To go to confession, we kneel in the confessional or go into the reconciliation room. In the room, we may either sit in front of Father or kneel next to him with a screen between us.

The priest might read a few sentences from God's book, the Bible. Then it will be time for us to say our sins.

The priest may ask some questions and give some advice. If something is bothering us, we can talk about it.

After this, the priest will give us a penance. (This is in the next lesson.) Then we will say a prayer of sorrow ("act of contrition"). For example, we may say the Jesus Prayer.

When the priest forgives our sins, we make the sign of the cross and say "Amen" at the end. We will know that God and God's people have forgiven us. What a happy moment!

Name

My Reconciliation
Booklet

Together, we praise God.
We thank Jesus for forgiving us.
We will tell others how good God is. His mercy endures forever!

1. cut here

4. cut here

We can come together to celebrate Penance and Reconciliation. We hear God's Word, calling us to live like Jesus. God's Word says: Love God. Love People.

3. fold here

I ask myself:

Do I love and thank God, who loves me?

What keeps me from praying to God?

Do I use God's name when I am surprised or angry?

Am I glad to go to Sunday or Saturday night Mass? If I miss Mass, what is the reason?

Do I obey my parents and teachers? Am I helpful at home?

What do I do when I feel angry? Have I looked for a way to hurt people I feel angry with?

Do I pick fights?

Do I treat my body with respect?

What kind of videos and TV shows do I watch?

Did I take and keep what belongs to someone else?

Did I break or ruin someone's things on purpose?

Do I tell the truth? Are my words helpful or hurtful?

Am I jealous of people's friends? Of their things?

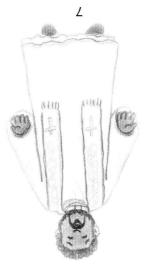

The priest gives me a penance.
I will do it, to show God I am
sorry for my sins.
I receive forgiveness from God
and the Church through the
words of the priest.

7

*Lord Jesus, Son of God, have
mercy on me, a sinner.*

Baptism made me God's child.
Jesus is my Brother and Savior!
The Holy Spirit lives in me!
I want to follow Jesus.
Sometimes, I am not like Jesus.
I make choices that do not
match God's plan.

2

It is my turn for confession.
The priest is there in Jesus'
place.
I tell him my sins. I tell him
how I try to follow Jesus.
I listen, too.

6

Sin makes me unhappy.
Sin hurts God's family
Jesus wants to forgive me.
God's family wants
to forgive me.
In Penance, I find forgiveness
from God and from the Church

3

We Choose

Which prayers of sorrow do you want to learn by heart?

We Grow

In the "Our Father" we pray: "Forgive us our trespasses as we forgive those who trespass against us." Why is it important to forgive people who have done wrong to us?

We Learn to Do Better

We Share

If someone had broken one of your toys, how could they show that they were sorry?

We Listen

When we go to confession, we say we are sorry. But we also need to *show* that we are sorry by trying to make up for our sins in some way.

If we broke something, we may have to fix it or buy another one to replace it. If we took something, we have to give it back. If we yelled at somebody, we have to say or show that we're sorry. If we told lies about somebody, we have to look for everybody who heard the lies and say that they weren't true.

We also have to say or do our *penance*. "Penance" means making up for something wrong that we have done. If we have been mean to a little brother for example, the priest may tell us to do an extra kind act for him. This sort of penance can help us learn to make better choices the next time. Most times the penance will be some prayers. When we pray them, we can tell God that we want to make up for our sins.

It is good to say these prayers as soon as we can, so we won't forget. Then we can also thank God for forgiving us. It is good to know that God loves us and is always ready to help and forgive us.

After our first Penance, we should try not to commit sins again. If possible, we should stay away from people, places and things that could make us want to do something wrong.

No matter how hard we try to avoid sin, we will commit venial sins sooner or later. It is good to make a plan for going to confession regularly. And if we do something really bad, we should go to confession as soon as we can.

Let us thank Jesus for giving us this wonderful way to stay close to him!

Saint John Vianney

St. John Vianney was a parish priest. He made sacrifices for people who were far from God.
When people confessed their sins to him, St. John was very gentle.
St. John Vianney helped many people to follow Jesus.

We Choose

Name a caring grown-up who will help you get to church for the sacrament of Penance.

We Grow

Once there were ten men with a bad skin disease called leprosy. They met Jesus on the road. They called out, "Jesus, teacher, help us!"

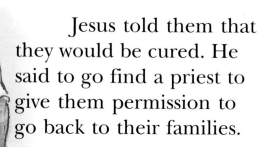

Jesus told them that they would be cured. He said to go find a priest to give them permission to go back to their families.

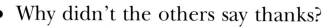

By the time the men found the priest, they had been cured! But only one of them came back to thank Jesus.

- Why didn't the others say thanks?
- How do you think Jesus felt about that?
- How will you show your thanks to God for the sacrament of Penance?

Choose the word that will complete
the sentence correctly.

1. ___penance___ means making up
for something wrong we have done.
(Penance Asking Prayers)

2. In confession, we say we are
___sorry___ for our sins.
(broken sorry quiet)

3. We ___show___ by our actions that
we are sorry for our sins.
(forget show ask)

4. With God's help, we try ___not___
to commit sins. (not more often)

5. When we do the ___penance___
the priest gives us in confession, we
learn to make better choices.
(song penance cross)

 will give
my life for
my sheep.
(John 10:15)

Part Three
Jesus Gives Himself to Us

We Give Thanks with Jesus

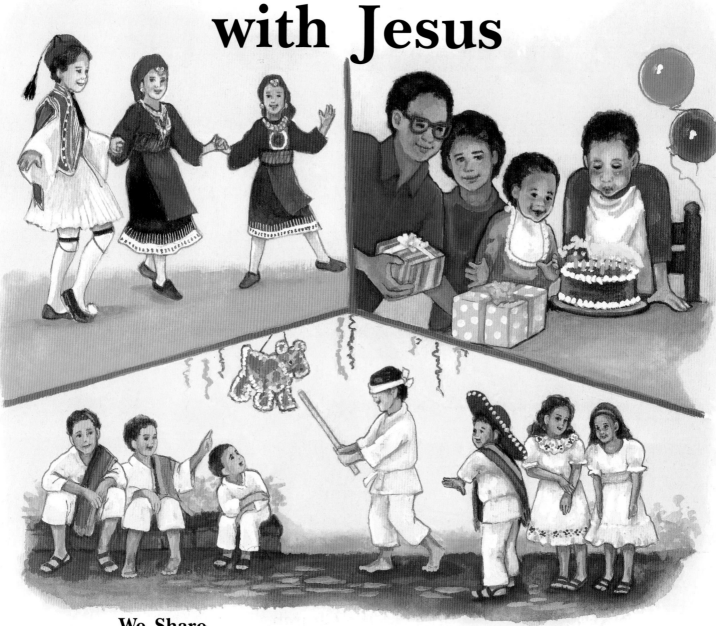

We Share

What does "celebration" mean? What celebrations do you like best?

We Listen

As members of the Church, we have a very special celebration. It is called the *Eucharist* or *Mass.*

The very first Eucharist took place the night before Jesus died. That evening, Jesus was eating supper with his friends, the apostles. The apostles were the first leaders of the Church.

Before Jesus passed the bread around, he thanked his Father for the gift of bread. Then he said, "Take this and eat it. This is my body." He also thanked his Father for the gift of wine. Then he passed a cup of wine around and said, "Take this and drink from it. This is my blood" (Mt. 26:26-28).

The apostles ate and drank. They could not see or taste anything different than bread and wine. But they believed what Jesus had said. They believed that instead of bread and wine, Jesus had given them his body and blood. The next day, Jesus would give his body and blood on the cross, by dying for us.

They remembered that Jesus had promised this. One time Jesus had said, "Anybody who eats my body and drinks my blood will live in me and will have life because of me. Anybody who eats this bread will live forever" (Jn. 6:56-58).

Jesus said something else to his friends: "Every time you do this, do it to remember me" (Lk. 22:19).

That was how the Eucharist began. The word "Eucharist" means "giving thanks." Jesus gave thanks to his Father at that special supper, the "Last Supper." At every Mass we remember what Jesus

did. We give thanks to God the Father for being so good to us. "God loved the world so much that he gave his only Son" (Jn. 3:16).

How good God has been to us!

Jesus Makes a Promise

Write "GIVE" or "GAVE" in the blanks to complete the sentence.

The bread I will _give_ is my flesh for the life of the world.

Jesus _gave_ thanks to God.

He _gave_ the people bread to eat.

We Choose

Where and when do you hear these words?
"For this is my Body."
"For this is the chalice of my Blood."

We Grow

When we eat this Bread and drink this Cup,
we proclaim your Death, O Lord,
until you come again.

Jesus Keeps His Promise

Write "GIVE" or "GAVE" in the blanks to complete the sentence.

Jesus _gave_ thanks to God.

He _gave_ the apostles his body and blood.

Jesus said, "Father, I _give_ my spirit over to you."

Jesus _gave_ his life for me.

Easter Is Our Biggest Celebration

We Share

How do you say that you love someone special?
How do you *show* that you love someone?

We Listen

For three years, Jesus had been telling people about God. His miracles showed God's love. His words told about it. Many people understood that God was with them in Jesus. But some of the leaders were jealous and afraid.

The day came to celebrate the Passover, when God saved his people from slavery. Jesus joined his friends for the special meal. His words and actions told them that God was going to save his people again. God would save them through Jesus. God would save them from sin. Jesus gave his apostles his own body and blood which he would offer on the cross to take away sin. That night, Jesus' enemies took him away.

Jesus knew that he was going to suffer and die for the people. He was ready for that. He trusted God his Father to make things work out.

On the cross, Jesus said, "Father, I put my life in your hands." Then he died. Mary his mother was so sad! Jesus' friends buried his body in a cave. There was no time for anything else.

On the third day, some women went to finish the funeral. Angels were there! The angels said, "Jesus is alive!" Then the women saw Jesus. Jesus said, "Peace! Do not be afraid. Go and tell the others the good news."

Jesus is risen! He lives with us!

A Put the events in order, then tell the story.

Jesus appears to the women. He is alive! Jesus brings us life!

For three years, Jesus teaches God's way and showsGod's love.

Jesus gives his life on the cross.

Jesus celebrates the Passover. He gives the apostles his body and blood.

Jesus' friends bury his body.

We Choose

Easter is a good time to remember our baptism.

We Grow

Imagine it is the first Easter. You were sad all weekend because Jesus died. Now the women have come to tell you that Jesus is risen. What would that news do for you? What does this news mean for you *today*?

St. Mary Magdalen

Mary Magdalen did not live God's way at first. Then she met Jesus. She believed in him. After that, Mary Magdalen followed Jesus. She stayed by him even when the others ran away. When Jesus rose, he sent Mary Magdalen and the other women to tell the apostles the Good News.

Solve the puzzles to finish the sentences.

1. _e u c h a r i s t_ means "giving thanks." (STEUCHARI)

2. We gather for Mass, and then we are _s e n t_ to share God's love. (NEST)

3. At the Last Supper, Jesus gave us the Eucharist. So we can call Mass the _L o r d_'s Supper. (DOLRS)

4. At Mass, we hear God's _w o r d_. (ROWD)

5. Our bread and wine become Christ's _b o d y_ and blood. (DOBY)

We Choose

What can you do to pray better at Mass?

We Grow

Jesus is with us at Mass!

St. Anne Line

St. Anne Line was a brave woman. In her country, it was against the law to be Catholic and go to Mass. But St. Anne told people to gather in secret. She helped priests come in for Mass. That is how St. Anne thanked Jesus for the gift of the Mass.

We Live by God's Word

We Share

What are some important things that you do during the week?

We Listen

In religion class we learn how to live the way Jesus asks us to. We also learn about this at Eucharist.

The first main part of the Mass is called the *Liturgy of the Word.* We listen to readings from God's book, the Bible. We call the Bible the Word of God, because in it God speaks to us.

"Liturgy" means "work done by the people." The most important "work" that God's people can do is to thank and pray to God.

In the Liturgy of the Word our main "work" is to listen to God and think how we can live by God's Word. Usually the priest or deacon will talk to us after he reads the Gospel. This talk helps us to see how to live by God's Word.

After the talk we say the Profession of Faith. This prayer is also called the Creed. In this prayer we say that we believe everything God has taught us and has done for us.

Then we pray for everybody.

We Choose

Here are some Mass responses you can learn:

Priest: The Lord be with you.
People: And with your spirit.

Reader: The word of the Lord.
People: Thanks be to God.

Priest: A reading from the holy Gospel
           according to N.
People: Glory to you, O Lord.

114

Name _____

We Hear GOD'S WORD at Mass

I believe in God
the Father almighty,
Creator of heaven and
earth.
I believe in Jesus Christ,
His only Son our Lord.
I believe in the Holy Spirit.
Lord, you will always hear
our prayer.

Glory to God in the highest!
Peace to his people on earth!

4

God spoke through
Moses and the prophets.
The people listened
and obeyed.
Thanks be to God!

5

1. cut here

2. fold here

7

Alleluia!
Jesus is God's Son!
He lived with us!
He taught us!
He died and rose to save us!
Praise to You, Lord Jesus Christ!

2

On Sunday, God's people come together.
We are joined by faith and baptism.
We gather to praise and thank God.

The apostles taught and wrote about God's Son. We listen to their words. *Thanks be to God!*

Lord, have mercy. *We do not always obey you.*
Christ, have mercy. *We do not always listen to you.*
Lord, have mercy. *Make us ready to listen to you and praise you!*

6

3

We Grow

If you were the reader for
Mass, what things would you
want to do so that everyone
could hear God's word?

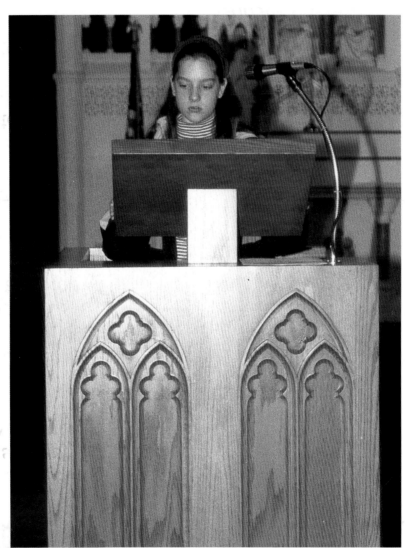

Lesson 19

Jesus Is Our Gift to God

We Share

On some holidays we remember things that happened in the past. Can you name some holidays like this?

We Listen

At Mass we remember something too, but in a different way. What we remember really comes into our lives.

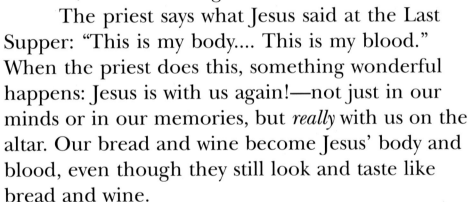

When Jesus died on the cross, he gave his life to God as a gift. This gift has a special name. It is called a "sacrifice," because it is a holy gift, a gift to God.

At Mass, the gift that Jesus gave to God, Jesus' sacrifice, becomes our gift to God too.

The priest says what Jesus said at the Last Supper: "This is my body.... This is my blood." When the priest does this, something wonderful happens: Jesus is with us again!—not just in our minds or in our memories, but *really* with us on the altar. Our bread and wine become Jesus' body and blood, even though they still look and taste like bread and wine.

At Mass, Jesus' gift to God is made present again and it becomes our gift too. At Mass, Jesus prays with us and for us to the Father. And the Holy Spirit helps us to pray to the Father with Jesus. With Jesus, we praise God who is so great and good. Everything we have is from God. With Jesus too, we ask God to forgive us and everybody. We ask for help so we can live as the children of God and the family of Jesus.

In Memory of Me

Use clues to fill in the blanks.

The bread becomes the <u>body</u> of Christ.

The wine becomes the <u>blood</u> of Christ.

Who said those words at the Last Supper?

(Fill in all the spaces with a • inside to find the answer.)

We Choose

Say the Great "Amen" at Mass as your *yes* to Jesus' sacrifice for you.

We Grow

What happened here?

What happened here?   122   What happens here?

our   bread   body   blood   wine   our   body

Use the word box to finish the sentences.
One is done for you.

1. At Mass, the b r e a d and w i n e become

   the body and blood of Christ.

2. The priest holds the bread. He says Jesus'

   words, "This is my b o d y."

3. At Mass, Jesus' sacrifice becomes o u r gift to God.

4. With Jesus o u r Savior, we praise God the Father.

5. Jesus gave his life for us. He gives us his

   b o d y and b l o o d in the Eucharist.

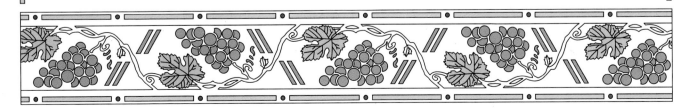

Jesus Is Our Holy Communion

We Share

Think about somebody you know well who is not here right now. Remember as much as you can about that person.

We Listen

When we remember somebody who is not with us, they become present to us *in spirit*. If that person came to see us, he or she would be with us *in body,* too.

Something like that happens at Mass.

At Mass Jesus is present in many ways. He is in his people, who have come to celebrate together. He is in his Word, the Bible, and he teaches us. He is in the priest, who says the words Jesus said at the Last Supper.

But when the priest says, "This is my body.... This is my blood," it is as if Jesus had been talking to us over the telephone and then suddenly came into the room. In the Eucharist, Jesus is present both in spirit and in body. That is why the Eucharist is so important to us.

We get ready to receive the Eucharist by praying the Our Father and giving a sign of peace to each other.

When we pray the Our Father, we remember that we are all children of God. That makes us brothers and sisters. In the sign of peace we show that we want to love all these brothers and sisters of ours.

Jesus will come to us in Communion. What we receive looks and tastes like bread. We might also receive what looks and tastes like wine. Either way, it's the whole Jesus who comes to us. We receive our brother and friend, who is also our God.

Jesus comes to make his life grow in us. He comes to give us love and make us strong in spirit. He comes to join all of God's people closer to him and to each other.

When you receive Communion, that will be a very good time to tell Jesus that you want to love him and everybody.

We Choose

Name some ways to show love and respect for Jesus' body and blood.

Name

**We Give Thanks
with Jesus**

8

With Jesus we thank God
our Father for all good gifts.
Like Jesus, we go to love
and serve God.

---

4. cut here

God has given us all
we have.
God has given us his
Son.
God has given us the
Holy Spirit.
We sing praise with
God's angels:
Holy, Holy, Holy Lord!

3. fold here

Jesus' words make his
sacrifice present.
**This is my body.
This is my blood.**

4

5

We receive Jesus with
love and respect.
Jesus is our friend and
Savior.

Our Father
who art in heaven,
hallowed be thy name.

Jesus is with us, his
people.
Jesus is with us, in his
Word.
Jesus is with us,
acting through the priest.

— 2. fold here —

Jesus is with us in the
Eucharist!
**Through him,
with him,
in him,
all glory to God!**
Amen!

We come together as
God's family
We hear God's words.
We bring gifts for
the poor.
We bring bread and wine
for the Mass.

We Grow

Practice the way to receive Holy Communion.
See pages 154 and 155.

Jesus Teaches Us to Pray

We Share

One day, Jesus' friends saw him praying to his Father. "Lord," they said, "teach us to pray, too" (Lk. 11:1).

- What did they want to know?
- Why is that important?

We Listen

Jesus taught us a special prayer to his Father. In this prayer we say that we care about God, others and ourselves. This prayer is the "Our Father," the Lord's Prayer:

> **Our Father who art in heaven,**
> **hallowed be thy name.**
> **Thy kingdom come.**
> **Thy will be done on earth, as it is in heaven.**
> **Give us this day our daily bread,**
> **and forgive us our trespasses,**
> **as we forgive those who trespass against us,**
> **and lead us not into temptation,**
> **but deliver us from evil.**
> **Amen.**

Jesus, God's Son became our Brother. Baptism made us all children of God in a special way: brothers and sisters of Jesus and of each other. That means that God is our Father! Of course, the word "Father" cannot tell us everything about God. God is different from any other father. God is greater and more wonderful than we can say in words.

The Lord's Prayer helps us remember that we are not alone. We pray to God, the Father of all. We pray for "our" daily bread and the forgiveness of "our" sins. This means that God's family, the Church, shares joys and sorrows. We pray for each other, forgive each other, help each other.

My First Communion

Tell about your First Communion.
Use the word box for ideas.

Word Box

~~Jesus~~   ~~Mass~~   body

~~first~~   ~~class~~

~~Word~~   Father

On (what day?) _Sunday_ I received (whom?)
Jesus for the _first_ time. I prepared for
this day with my _class_. Other people helped me,
too (name two of them): _Melissa_ and
Maria Mansella.

My First Communion was at (which parish?)
St. Thomas Apostle.

At _Mass_ we heard God's _word_. We prayed
together. The priest took bread and wine. He said
the same words _____ said at the Last Supper.
The bread and wine became the _____ and blood
of Christ. We prayed, "Our _____ who art in
heaven." We received the Eucharist, the Body of
Christ. Everyone had time to thank _____ for
coming in Holy Communion. Now I can receive
Communion at every _____.

We Choose

The Church prays the Our Father at Mass
and other important times.
When will *you* pray it?

We Grow

Imagine your favorite place. There you see Jesus! He is praying. You go near, and Jesus welcomes you. "Jesus, teach me how to pray, too," you say. In the stillness of your heart, listen to the way Jesus prays with you. Stay with him as long as you like.

The Church Prays the Our Father

- in the morning

- at Mass

- at night

Draw yourself praying the Our Father with God's people at Mass.

Pentecost Is a Day of Joy

We Share

Have you ever had big news that you just couldn't keep inside of you?

We Listen

For forty days after he rose from the dead, Jesus' followers would see him from time to time. They enjoyed these visits with the Risen Jesus. It was not like before, because Jesus was not always visible. But he seemed to be always with them. Then it was time for Jesus to go to his Father. He told his followers to stay together and pray. Jesus was going to ask the Father to send the Holy Spirit to them.

Jesus' followers went to the city to pray together. Mary was with them. They waited for nine days. Then, while they were praying, there was the sound of a big wind inside the house. They saw flames of fire in the air. They felt the Holy Spirit in their hearts. They shouted out loud for joy! Then they went outside to tell all the people about Jesus. "God has kept his promise," Peter told the crowds.

"What should we do?" a man asked.

"Be sorry for your sins," Peter said, "and be baptized. You will receive the Holy Spirit, too!" That day, thousands of people did what Peter said.

Ever since that Pentecost day, the Church has been telling people about Jesus. It is the Holy Spirit who tells the Church what to say. It is the Holy Spirit who helps people believe the good news and come for baptism. It is the Holy Spirit who helps people live like Jesus.

We cannot see the Holy Spirit with our eyes. We cannot hear the Holy Spirit with our ears. But the Holy Spirit is always helping the Church. That is why Pentecost is a day of joy!

The Risen Jesus Returned to His Father.

De-code!

Jesus said:
I MA TIWH OUY
WALYAS.

Draw a cloud beneath Jesus' feet.

Look carefully in the picture. Find some of the ways Jesus is with us:

- in God's Word
- in God's people
- in the priest
- in the Eucharist

We Choose

On Pentecost Sunday, look at the vestments the priest wears for Mass. They are red, like the flames of fire on the first Pentecost, or like hearts full of love for Jesus.

We Grow

Why is it important for people to learn about Jesus and about God's love?

If you were Peter, what would you say to the people about Jesus? (Ask the Holy Spirit to help you.)

The Holy Spirit Is with the Church

Draw a flame of fire over each person's head to show the "fire" of God's Holy Spirit.

 will bless
the Lord
at all
times.
(Psalm 34:1)

Special Sessions

Jesus Is Coming

When our first parents turned away from God, God did not turn away from them. God still loved them, and promised to save them.

One whole part of the Bible is about God's people waiting to see God's promise. No one knew when or how God would save his people. No one knew who the savior would be. God gave hints, but he kept the rest secret until the right time came. When sad things happened to the people, God would give more hints, so the people would not give up hope. "I will save you myself," God said.

For many long years, the people waited. Then one night, angels told the news: "A savior has been born!" God's own Son had come to save the people! He was named Jesus. This name means "God saves."

We know that Jesus has come. He saved us through his dying and rising. Now Jesus comes to us in the sacraments and through other people. One day, Jesus will come in a big way. Then there will be no more sin, harm or hurt in the whole world. All creation will praise and thank God for his saving deeds. This is what we are waiting for. This is what we are asking for when we pray, "Thy kingdom come."

Getting Ready for Jesus

Connect the dots to finish each picture.

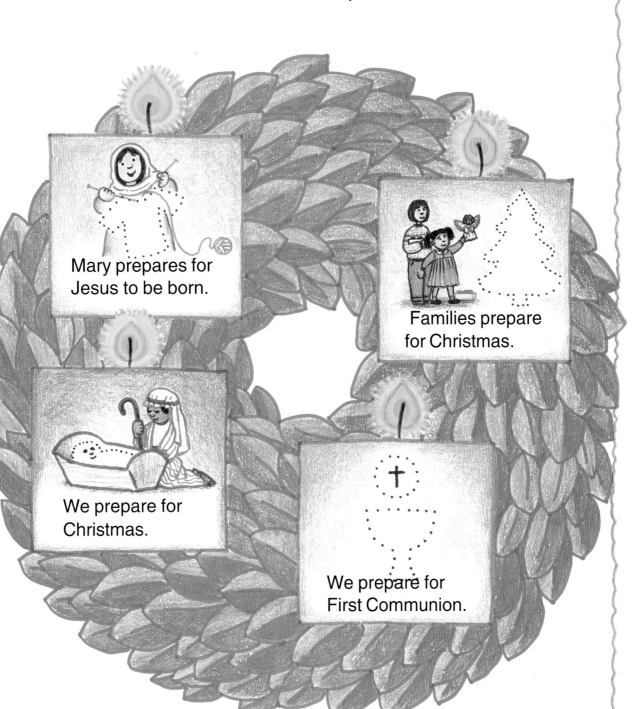

Mary prepares for Jesus to be born.

Families prepare for Christmas.

We prepare for Christmas.

We prepare for First Communion.

We Grow in Lent

God's people had been slaves, but through Moses, God set them free. Then God led them home across the desert. It was a long trip. The people got tired and hungry. They even got angry at God!

God did not stop loving his people. There in the desert, God gave them bread called manna. God gave them wise laws, the commandments. God promised to always be their God. During their trip, the people became like a family. And after a long time, they came home to the Promised Land.

Jesus spent a long time in the desert once, too. For forty whole days, he stayed in the lonely desert to pray. When his desert time was over, Jesus was ready to start his saving work.

Lent is the Church's desert time. It is a journey to Easter. During Lent, many people are getting ready for baptism. They will become members of the Church at Easter. We help these people prepare for baptism. In Lent, we try harder to live like Jesus. We pray more. We do penance. We look for extra ways to show kindness. God helps us.

This desert time brings the Church closer together.

146

Lenten Journey Map

Decide on a special way you will keep Lent. It can be a prayer, a good deed, or a sacrifice. Write it here:

MY LENTEN PLAN

_____

Follow Jesus to *EASTER LIFE!*

Each day you keep your Lenten Plan, put a purple border around the box.

			Lent begins **Ash Wednesday**	Make a list of people to pray for.	For the Holy Father, today I will: _____	In Lent, many people will prepare for baptism.
Food is not enough to keep people alive: we need God's Word, too.	Do a secret favor for someone.	unscramble: SUJES SI ROU NOLY VASIOR.	During Lent, I will pray for those who are preparing for Baptism.		Use your prayer list tonight when you pray.	For the sick and elderly, today I will: _____
Jesus is God's beloved Son. I will listen to him.	What ways can you help the poor during this Lent?	Enjoy a good book today!	Which two are alike?	By Baptism, you became God's adopted child!		Does someone need my smile today?
Make up a poem about God's love.	For my friends, today I will:	de-code: ESJUS, I VOLE UOY!	Do a kindness for someone hard to like.		For my teachers, today I will:	Mary, help me to love my neigh-bor.
Pray today the prayer you love best.	I will ask Jesus to help me always tell the truth!		For all the children in the world, today I will: _____	decode: SEJUS VIESL NI EM!	Today, watch one less TV show than usual, and read a good story instead.	Can you explain to a friend what Lent means?
Write a special "grace before meals" and pray it tonight at supper!	Write a letter from Jesus to you. Keep it in a special place.	For my parents, today I will: _____		Color the stained glass!	For all the poor, today I will: _____	Name some ways you can come closer to Jesus.
Passion Sunday Hosanna!	This is a very special week.	I will walk with Jesus each day.	Jesus, stay always in my heart!	**EASTER THREE-DAYS** **Holy Thursday** Thank you, Jesus, for the Mass!	**Good Friday** Jesus died for me.	**Easter Vigil** Stay close to Mary as you wait for Easter joy.

How to Celebrate the Sacrament of Penance

Preparing for Confession

First, ask God to help you to know what sins you have committed and to be sorry for them. You might say this prayer:

God the Father, Son, and Holy Spirit, I know that you love me. I have not always loved you back. Help me to know my sins and be sorry for them. Help me to want to be better. Mary, Mother of Jesus and my Mother, please give me your help, too.

Then ask yourself what you have thought, said, done, or failed to do which did not match God's loving plan. You don't have to remember everything.

These questions may help you.

About loving God:

Did I turn my mind away from God on purpose and without a good reason while I was praying?

Did I on purpose and without a good reason distract other people when they were praying?

Did I use God's name or Jesus' name when surprised or angry?

Did I miss Mass on Sundays (or on Saturday nights, which count as Sundays) through *my* own fault, and without a very good reason?

Did I come late to Mass on these days through my own fault?

Do I go to Mass gladly, or do grown-ups have to make me go?

Do I invite others to come for Mass?

About loving myself and others:

Did I disobey my parents or teachers?

Did I talk back to them?

Did I make fun of old people?

What do I do when I feel angry?

Did I fight?

Was I mean to anyone on purpose? Why?

Did I keep mean thoughts in my mind on purpose?

Did I try out drugs or alcohol?

Did I call other people names?

Did I follow people who do bad things?

Did I say bad words?

Did I on purpose watch programs in which the talk or actions were bad?

Do I treat my body with respect, because it is holy?

Do I treat other people's bodies with reverence?

Did I steal? Did I tell someone else to steal?

Did I cheat?

Did I keep something that wasn't mine?

Did I share with others when I could?

Did I destroy other people's things on purpose—breaking toys, ruining clothes, writing on walls or buildings?

Did I harm God's creation on purpose by dumping trash or hurting animals?

Did I tell lies? Did these lies hurt other people?

Am I jealous of other people's friends? of their things?

Do I do mean things because I am jealous?

Tell God how sorry you are for the ways you have failed to love. Think of the way you can do better, and promise God that with his help, you will do it.

Going to Confession

When your turn comes, you go into the confessional or the room. The priest welcomes you. You make the sign of the cross. Father says a little prayer for you. You answer: **Amen.**

Father may read to you from God's Book, the Bible.

This reading helps you to remember how much God loves you and how forgiving God is.

Now you say: **Father, this is my first confession,** or: **Father, it has been** (how long?) **since my last confession.**

You say your sins, starting with the ones you think were the biggest.

Father talks to you. (You ask questions if you have any.)

Father gives you a penance—something to say or do to make up a little for your sins.

You say an act of contrition, which means a prayer of sorrow. In an act of contrition we tell God that we are sorry and will try to do better, and we mean it.

Now Father says the words which bring you Jesus' forgiveness. At the same time, he may hold his hand over your head. These are the words that the priest says:

> God, the Father of mercies,
> through the death and resurrection of his Son
> has reconciled the world to himself
> and sent the Holy Spirit among us
> for the forgiveness of sins;
> through the ministry of the Church
> may God give you pardon and peace,
> and I absolve you from your sins
> in the name of the Father, and of the Son,
> and of the Holy Spirit.

You make the sign of the cross and answer: **Amen.**
Father says: Give thanks to the Lord, for he is good.
You answer: **His mercy endures forever.** (This means that God always forgives us if we are sorry.)

Then Father tells you to go in peace. You may answer: **Amen** or: **Thank you, Father.**

What to Do after Confession

Say or do your penance right away or as soon as possible. It is also good to say a little prayer of gratitude, such as:

Thank You, Jesus, for forgiving me. Please help me keep my promise to you and to try to be good.

What We See and Do at Mass

What the Priest Wears

We all have important things to do at Mass, but the priest has a very special part. We can easily pay attention to what the priest is doing, because he wears special clothes. These clothes are called vestments. Vestments have different shapes and designs. They also have different colors.

Green is the color that is used most of the time.

White is used in the Christmas Season and Easter Season. It is also used for celebrations that honor Jesus, Mary or some of the saints.

Violet is usually used in Advent and Lent.

Red is used on Palm Sunday and Good Friday and in Masses that honor the Holy Spirit or the saints called martyrs.

What the Priest Uses

The lector and the priest or deacon read God's Word, the Bible, from this big book.

This cup and these bowls are for the bread that becomes Jesus' body.

The priest reads prayers from another big book.

These pitchers are for water and wine. During the Mass the priest adds a little water to the wine.

This cup is for the wine that becomes Jesus' blood.

These cups are for receiving Jesus' blood under the appearance of wine.

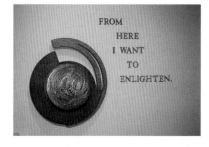

The tabernacle is where the Eucharist stays after Mass, so Christ's Body can be brought to the sick.

How to Receive Communion

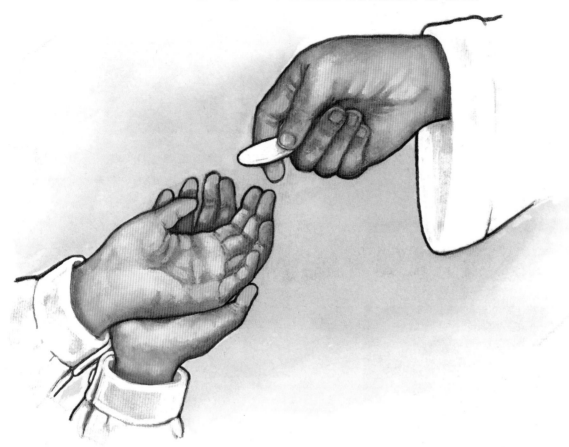

Your teacher, parent or guardian will help you learn this.

To receive Communion in your *hand,* cross your hands with the palms upward. Make a cup of your upper hand. The priest or eucharistic minister will say, "Body of Christ." Answer "Amen." "Amen" means "Yes. It's true!" After the Host has been placed in your hand, step to the side and stand still. Pick up the Host, and put It in your mouth. Swallow the Host. Then go back to your pew.

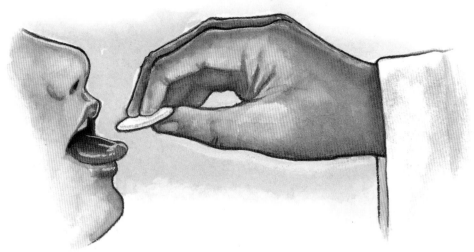

To receive Communion on your *tongue,* answer "Amen" after the priest or eucharistic minister says, "Body of Christ." Put your tongue out as far as you can. Hold your tongue steady until the Host has been placed on it. Then swallow the Host.

To receive Communion from the chalice, answer "Amen" after the priest or eucharistic minister says, "Blood of Christ." Drink a little from the chalice. Jesus is there under the appearance of wine.

Before Communion we do not eat or drink anything except water for at least an hour. This is a way of showing respect for Jesus.

We genuflect before the Eucharist to show honor to Jesus Christ.

LET'S TALK

Sign of the Cross

In the name of the
   Father,
and of the Son,
and of the Holy Spirit.
Amen.

Hail Mary

Hail, Mary, full of grace!
The Lord is with you.
Blessed are you among
   women,

Glory

Glory to the Father,
and to the Son,
and to the Holy Spirit:
as it was in the beginning,
is now,
and will be for ever.
Amen.

Our Father

Our Father, who art in
   heaven,
hallowed be thy name.
Thy kingdom come.
Thy will be done
   on earth
as it is in heaven.
Give us this day
our daily bread,
and forgive us our
   trespasses,
as we forgive those
who trespass against us.
And lead us not into
   temptation;
but deliver us from evil.
Amen.

TO GOD

and blessed is the fruit
of your womb, Jesus.
Holy Mary, Mother of
    God
pray for us sinners now
    and at the hour
of our death.
Amen.

Grace Before Meals

Lord God,
bless us
and the good food
you have given us.
Amen.

Grace After Meals

Lord God,
thank you
for all the good things
you do for us.
Amen.

Two Prayers of Sorrow

Act of Contrition

My God, I am sorry
    for my sins
with all my heart.
In choosing to to wrong
and failing to do good,
I have sinned against you
whom I should love
    above all things.
I firmly intend,
    with your help.
to do penance,
    to sin no more,
and to avoid whatever
    leads me to sin.
Our Savior Jesus Christ
suffered and died for us
in his name, my God,
have mercy.

Jesus Prayer

Lord Jesus, Son of God,
have mercy on me,
    a sinner

Glossary

Part 1

Baptism—a sign of Jesus' love in which he gives us his life (grace) and makes us members of his Church through water and special words.

Bible—the book in which God speaks to us: God's Word.

Church—the family of Jesus; people joined to him by grace and/or Baptism.

Eucharist—the great sign of Jesus' love in which Jesus makes his sacrifice present and feeds us with his body and blood.

grace—a share in God's own life.

heaven—happiness with God forever.

Mary—the mother of Jesus. Because Jesus is true God and true man, Mary is called "Mother of God."

miracle—a wonderful happening that can take place only through God's power.

Penance—a sign (a sacrament) of Jesus' love in which we find forgiveness from God and the Church for sins committed after Baptism.

pray—talk and listen to God or to his friends in heaven.

psalm—a song-prayer from the Bible.

sacrament—a celebration of the Church in which the Holy Spirit shares God's life with us; they give us God's own life and help so we can live as better Christians.

Part 2

adultery—unfaithfulness to marriage vows.

bear false witness—to lie.

commandments—rules that God gave us to help us be happy.

confession—telling our sins to the priest in the sacrament of Penance.

contrition—sorrow for sins.

covet—to want something that belongs to someone else; to be jealous.

in vain—without a serious reason; uselessly.

neighbor—any other person.

penance—something to say or do to make up for sins.

priest—a man to whom Jesus gives power to act for him in offering the Mass and forgiving sins.

Reconciliation—the sacrament of Penance, of God's loving forgiveness.

sin—saying "no" to Jesus' way of living; turning away from a chance to love.

strange gods—created things that we give too much honor to.

the Lord's Day—a day set apart to honor God and to relax. Followers of Jesus observe Sunday as the Lord's Day.

Part 3

apostles—special friends of Jesus who became leaders in the early Church.

Communion—receiving the body and blood of Christ.

Eucharistic Celebration—another name for the Mass.

Gospel—the part of the Bible that tells what Jesus did and said.

Last Supper—the last meal Jesus ate with his friends before he died.

Liturgy—"work done by the people" to serve God—especially by praising and thanking God.

Lord's Supper—a name that reminds us that Jesus gave us the Eucharist at the last meal he shared with his friends.

Mass—the sacrifice-meal of Jesus' family, the Church. At Mass, God's people listen to God's Word, offer Jesus to the Father and receive Holy Communion, then are sent to share God's love with others.

Pentecost—the day the Church celebrates the coming of the Holy Spirit.

proclaim—announce; read with expression.

Special/Seasonal Sessions

Advent—the time of preparing for Christmas.

Lent—the time of preparing for Easter.

Yuvati

Pauline
BOOKS & MEDIA

The Daughters of St. Paul operate book and media centers at the following addresses. Visit, call or write the one nearest you today, or find us at www.pauline.org.

CALIFORNIA
3908 Sepulveda Blvd, Culver City, CA 90230 — 310-397-8676
935 Brewster Avenue, Redwood City, CA 94063 — 650-369-4230
5945 Balboa Avenue, San Diego, CA 92111 — 858-565-9181

FLORIDA
145 S.W. 107th Avenue, Miami, FL 33174 — 305-559-6715

HAWAII
1143 Bishop Street, Honolulu, HI 96813 — 808-521-2731

ILLINOIS
172 North Michigan Avenue, Chicago, IL 60601 — 312-346-4228

LOUISIANA
4403 Veterans Memorial Blvd, Metairie, LA 70006 — 504-887-7631

MASSACHUSETTS
885 Providence Hwy, Dedham, MA 02026 — 781-326-5385

MISSOURI
9804 Watson Road, St. Louis, MO 63126 — 314-965-3512

NEW YORK
64 W. 38th Street, New York, NY 10018 — 212-754-1110

TEXAS
Currently no book center; for parish exhibits or outreach evangelization, contact: 210-569-0500, or SanAntonio@paulinemedia.com, or P.O. Box 761416, San Antonio, TX 78245

SOUTH CAROLINA
243 King Street, Charleston, SC 29401 — 843-577-0175

VIRGINIA
1025 King Street, Alexandria, VA 22314 — 703-549-3806

CANADA
3022 Dufferin Street, Toronto, Ontario, Canada M6B 3T5 — 416-781-9131

¡También somos su fuente para libros,
videos y música en español!